Shipwrecked Faith

Breaking Free From The Bondage of Religion

Heather Evans

Kingdom Reign Publishing

Published First Edition: Kingdom Reign Publishing

Contact: https://travisandtiffanytombre.com/kingdomreignpublishing/

Author Photo: Heather Evans

Cover Layout and Manuscript Formatting: Tiffany Tombre

ISBN: 979-8-9926890-0-6

PRINTED IN THE UNITED STATES OF AMERICA

Contents

About the Author

Heather Evans

Acknowledgements

I want to acknowledge my Heavenly Father for allowing me to write this book. During the process, I never called it my book but His. He used me to write to His people. I want to acknowledge my husband, Jimmie, and children, Trystan, Wyatt, and Piper, for their support and encouragement through this process. I am so thankful Abba put each of you in my life and allowed me to be your wife and mother. It is a calling I will never take for granted. I also want to acknowledge my wonderful publisher, Tiffany Tombre, for her guidance and patience in the writing process. If you are interested in writing a book of your own, I highly recommend that you contact her at https://travisandtiffanytombre.com/kingdomreignpublis hing/

Dedication

I WANT TO DEDICATE this book to you! To those who love the Lord and want to learn how to walk closer to Him and better understand His Word and who He is. To those who desire more out of life and are ready to be free from the enemy on all sides. To those struggling with their prayer life and don't know where to begin. God's love for you is boundless, and it is time to receive what He has had for you all along.

Introduction

This charge I entrust to you, Timothy my son, in keeping with the prophecies once spoken about you, so that by them you fight the good fight, holding onto faith and a good conscience. By rejecting these, some have suffered shipwreck regarding their faith. **1 Timothy 1:18-19 TLV**

I WANT TO DIG into the part of 1 Timothy 1:18-19 that says to hold onto faith and a good conscience.

Hold onto your faith. Cling to it and do not let go. I heard this analogy once about a person drowning, clinging to a life preserver waiting to be rescued, clinging to it as if their life depended on it. That is the perfect analogy for your faith. Cling to it with that kind of desperation because that is all that will matter at the end of your life. Cling to your faith, not your religion.

From a biblical view, a good conscience is an inner sense of right and wrong placed there by God. You get to choose which path you will follow. He is a God of free will and will never force us to follow Him. He wants you to *want* to follow Him.

If we do not trust God's Word or choose to follow it, we will violate our conscience, resulting in the shipwreck of our faith. This book will focus on religion. Religion has shipwrecked so many people's faith and blinded so many of God's people, and I wanted to expose it for what it really is—deception! God does not want His people to capsize and stay in bondage to the enemy. He wants you free. God does not want your faith shipwrecked.

It is about a relationship, not religion. God wants a personal relationship with you. You will not get to Heaven, stand before Him, and be asked what you did for your religion; He will ask what you did for Him.

> *For it is written, "As I live, says ADONAI, every knee shall bow to Me, and every tongue shall give praise to God." So then each one of us shall give account of himself to God. Romans 14:11-12 TLV*

I pray you will allow the words in this book to shift your perspective, transform your life, and break you from bondage and that, by the last chapter, you will be fully walking in freedom and seeking after your Heavenly Father as you have never done before. This is a call-to-action book! There will be decrees, declarations, and prayers at the end of some of the chapters. What that means is when you read those out loud, you are verbally, with your own mouth, declaring freedom from the bondage of religion. There is power in speaking prayer out loud, not just in your head. You will recognize it, acknowledge it, come out of agreement with it, and commit to change moving forward. Do not skip over them, even if finishing one chapter takes days or weeks! I want you to understand what God has for you in these pages. As you say the prayers out loud, believe what you are saying, and don't doubt! Trust that your Heavenly Father has gone before you.

> *But let him ask in faith, without any doubting—for the one who doubts is like a wave of the sea, blown and tossed by the wind. For that person must not suppose that he will receive anything from the Lord— he is a double-minded man, unstable in all his ways. James 1:6-8 TLV*

I encourage you to pull your Bible out while reading this book.

Side note: You will see me use God's names often. I encourage you to look them up and note them and their meaning. I have included some of them below for you.

In this book, I will refer to Jesus as Yeshua (yeh-shoo-uh) because that is His Hebrew/Aramaic name. Anytime you see Yeshua, know I'm talking about Jesus.

Before you start each chapter, there will be suggested readings to help you better understand where I'm going with that message. It isn't required but will help you dive deeper into the Word.

Names of God with Meaning:

-Abba – Father

-Alpha and Omega – The Beginning and the End

-Elohim- Mighty Creator

-El Shaddai- God Almighty

-El Elyon- Most High God

-El Olam – Everlasting God

-El Roi- The God Who Sees

-Jehovah Rapha- The Lord Who Heals

-Jehovah Shalom- The Lord is Peace

-Jehovah Jireh – The Lord Will Provide

-Yahweh- He Brings Into Existence Whatever Exists

Chapter One

It All Started with a Dream

"In a dream, in a vision of the night, when deep sleep falls on men, as they slumber in bed, Then He opens the ears of men and seals their instruction, in order to turn a man from his conduct and to cover a person's pride." Job 33:15-17 TLV

'And it shall be in the last days,' says God, 'that I will pour out My Ruach on all flesh. Your sons and your daughters shall prophesy, your young men shall see visions, and your old men shall dream dreams.' Acts 2:17 TLV

DREAMS ARE JUST AS much for today as for the Old and New Testaments. They are such a beautiful gift from our Heavenly Father. He uses them because when we are asleep, our minds are quiet, and we are still. It is one way Abba communicates with us. I want to share one of my dreams that shifted everything and woke me up spiritually. It is the reason God had me write this book. This is how it went...

I was in a small country church. There were about 10 to 14 old-style wooden pews lined with people. They were all smiling and seemed to be having an enjoyable time, but something was off to me. I walked up to the married couple sitting in the back row, and they were talking about God's love. After talking to them more, I realized they only knew of His love. Not His wrath, His commandments, having a relationship with Him, nothing. I do not even think they realized they were sinners and needed to repent. Then, the pastor got on the platform and discussed God's love again.

Nothing else! I knew then that he was in it for show, not for bringing God's people closer to Him. He was not shepherding his flock. He entertained them to keep them happy. A happy congregation sees him, the pastor, as their savior. They worshipped him. They hung on every word he said as if it was the whole truth, but sadly, I was the only one there who knew it was not. He was a cotton candy pastor. He was sugarcoating his flock, and they did not know any better. Then I was upstairs looking down at the platform. A kid dressed like Alfalfa from *The Little Rascals* sang a worldly song. The congregation was all giddy, excited, and just oohing and ahhing over this kid. They were going through the motions of a Sunday service and trusting their pastor to get them to Heaven. They were good people, so surely God would let them in.

My heart broke. I woke up crying the deepest cry that I ever had at that point in my life. My Spirit was heavy.

I took off to the bathroom so as not to wake my husband, closed the door, and sat down. I immediately asked for an answer from God. I prayed hard. I cried out, "Father, what was that? What did you want me to see?" I felt the Father say, "This is an ounce of My heart for My people. My people do not know Me."

Like the people in my dream, are you just going through the motions? Are you just there to be entertained, to mark it off your list of things to do to be "holy and good?" Do you know Him, and does He know you?

"My sheep hear My voice. I know them, and they follow Me." John 10:27 TLV

Many believers will not make it to Heaven because they never took the time to know Him. They did not accept Yeshua into their hearts, or the Yeshua that they received was not the one true Yeshua. It is one thing to believe in Him. It is quite another to follow Him. Even demons believe in Him but do not follow Him; there is a big difference. If you are a follower of Yeshua, this scripture should make you aware of the seriousness of Heaven and Hell.

Not everyone who says to Me, 'Lord, Lord!' will enter the kingdom of heaven, but he who does the will of My Father in heaven. Many will say to Me on that day, 'Lord, Lord, didn't we prophesy in Your name, and drive out demons in Your name, and perform many miracles in Your name?' Then I will declare to them, 'I never knew you. Get away from Me, you workers of lawlessness!' Matthew 7:21-23 TLV

Do you want more of God? Do you want to live in the fullness of what He has for you? There is so much more. If He is tugging you for more, do not hesitate. Respond! I pray this book helps you leave religion behind, that it exposes the lies you have been believing, replaces them with God's truth, and motivates you to have an intimate relationship with your Heavenly Father. He is waiting and longing for you to know who He is.

"But from there you will seek Adonai your God and you will find Him when you seek Him with all your heart and with all your soul." Deuteronomy 4:29 TLV

"As the deer pants for streams of water, so my soul pants for You, O God." Psalm 42:2 TLV

Pray Out Loud:

Father, as I begin a new journey of learning about the religious spirit and how to break free from it, please open my spiritual eyes and ears so I can see and hear You clearly during this process. Help me not to shut down any new ideas and start with a clean slate. Give me Your wisdom and knowledge. Help me retain the information and apply it to my life. Learning new things isn't always easy. I believe You will go before me and make it all make sense. Expose any lies I believe and help me release them to You as You reveal them to me. I want to know more about You—who you really are! Thank you, Father. In the mighty name of Yeshua, Amen.

Chapter Two

Now You Can Go

Suggested Reading: Matthew 10 & John 14

"The reason the world is not seeing Jesus is that Christian people are not filled with Jesus. They are satisfied with attending meetings weekly, reading the Bible occasionally, and praying sometimes. It is an awful thing for me to see people who profess to be Christians lifeless, powerless, and in a place where their lives are so parallel to unbelievers' lives that it is difficult to tell which place they are in, whether in the flesh or in the Spirit." Smith Wigglesworth

I'm going to share a little bit of my history with religion. I was raised Catholic, but when I graduated high school in 2003, I took a long break from God. I felt something pulling me back to church, so my husband and I ended up at a non-denominational church in 2008. Being surrounded by every religion on every corner, we decided that the church we picked was best for our family at the time. Fast forward to 2022, I felt a hard tug to go deeper with God. I committed more time to Him as He asked. Never ignore His tug! I committed more time to prayer and was intentional about studying the Word. Not just reading it but studying it. The Holy Spirit is a better teacher than any man ever will be! You don't need all the devotionals or books to tell you who He is. They are great and can give you insight to dive deeper, but you should fully rely on the written Word alone.

> *"But the Helper, the Ruach ha-Kodesh whom the Father will send in My name, will teach you everything and remind you of everything that I said to you." John 14:26 TLV*

Over that year, God showed me that there was more He had for me than just where I was, but I had to be willing to move out of my comfort zone to get it. I didn't know what that meant at the time. In 2023, I started speaking in tongues. I was under spiritual attack, and a friend asked me if I spoke in tongues. I have always been taught it was a gift for certain people, but I never thought it could be for me. I didn't know that it was a gift for all believers. Here are a few scriptures for you to dig into.

> *"For one who speaks in a tongue speaks not to people but to God—for no one understands, but in the Spirit he speaks mysteries." 1 Corinthians 14:2 TLV*

"These signs will accompany those who believe: in My name they will drive out demons; they will speak new languages."Mark 16:17a TLV

The church I was attending that year was against speaking in tongues, and I wondered, if the Bible never said that speaking in tongues is extinct, then why does the church not allow it and say it isn't for our time? I remember how excited I was about it but also scared to mention it to anyone there for fear of rejection. I didn't want them to discredit God's actions in and through me, so I kept quiet. Little did I know that from September to December 2023, God would completely flip my entire world upside down. I remember walking into that church sanctuary one day just talking to the Lord, and I felt like I wanted to speak in tongues. I heard this voice stop me and say, "I'm not welcome here." I immediately felt this weight, this heaviness in my Spirit. I heard God tell me to leave that church shortly after, but I questioned it. It had to have been my own voice because why would God ask me to leave His church? Then He said again, "It is time for you to leave this church." He didn't want me or my family to be a part of a church that didn't allow the Holy Spirit to move. The more you obey Him, the more He opens your eyes to His ways.

Over the next week, I went to my prayer room and asked God to show me where He wanted me to go or if He wanted me to start a home church. I saw this Matthew scripture and realized He wanted me connected to a church that walked in these functions:

"Heal the sick, raise the dead, cleanse those with leprosy, drive out demons. Freely you received, freely give. As

you go, proclaim, 'The kingdom of heaven has come near!'" Matthew 10:7-8 TLV

That verse is an active command from Yeshua Himself, not only for the people back then but also for us today.

That was at the end of October. Soon after, He showed me what church He wanted me to attend. They hosted a revival that weekend, so my husband and I attended. When I entered the door, God said, "This is your home." I felt it, too! I felt overwhelmed with joy and completion.

After that, I foolishly started negotiating with God. I was leading a ladies' Bible study group at my church and didn't want to leave because I had no one to replace me, so I figured I would wait until April to leave for good when the classes would break for summer. I had the whole plan ready. Attend that church every other Sunday and the new church in between that. I thought that was a good balance, but God wasn't pleased with that plan. Looking back, I see He was also trying to protect me from bitterness. Shortly after that, I met with two church leaders and was asked to resign from leading.

Not because I did anything wrong but because I didn't claim their religion. Right after they mentioned me stepping down, I heard God say loud and clear, "Now You Can Go!" In my prayer time the following day, God told me never to step foot in that church again, and I can honestly say I obeyed Him. I asked God why I had to leave, and He said I had to leave so He could get me where He wanted me to be: equipped and prepared for what was coming. My heart broke, and I grieved, but I obeyed my Heavenly Father. I miss the people! I really do. When I say He was saving me from bitterness, I found out two of the ladies I thought were my friends were spreading rumors about me shortly after that. It hurt my heart.

I don't think a friend has ever hurt me like that. I wanted to call both of them and set them straight, but the Lord said to be quiet, and He would handle it. I did exactly as I was told. Vengeance belongs to the Lord, not me. I have forgiven them both, which took a while, and He has been faithful in replacing them with people who are after His heart, which I needed in my life.

We started actively attending the new church in January. In a very short time, God broke the spirit of fear off me. I no longer have the spirit of anxiety and depression. I am free! If I had stayed in religion, I would still be sitting in fear and bondage from the enemy. That was never God's plan for me or you, and where you attend church matters! I heard this saying once that when you get to Heaven, and God is asking you questions, He isn't going to ask about religion. He is going to ask about your relationship with Him. Do you have a relationship with God? If not, now is the time to start.

In this book, I will walk you through how to have an intimate relationship with your Heavenly Father.

"For God has not given us a spirit of timidity but of power and love and self-discipline." 2 Timothy 1:7 TLV

Chapter Three
The Spirit of Religion

SUGGESTED READING: MARK 7 & 2 Timothy 3

"The religious spirit is the author of cessationism, a doctrine of demons that says the gifts of the Holy Spirit are not for today." Jeremiah Johnson

This chapter will be deeper than the previous chapters. It will challenge what you have been taught your entire life. It will shift your mind and heart if you allow it. It will require you to decide what you will continue to believe. Since we are going deeper, let's pray so you don't miss anything God has for you.

Pray Out Loud:

Father, open my eyes and ears from the deepest depths within me so I can see and hear what You are trying to say in this chapter. Soften my heart and remove any blocks from the enemy trying to keep me from learning Your truth. As I read this chapter, silence the distractions and the noise around me. Thank you, Father. In Yeshua's mighty name, Amen.

The spirit of religion is a demonic spirit that influences people to replace their relationship with God with traditions and works, which you see very much today. Many churches today focus more on the business of Yeshua instead of focusing on Yeshua Himself. This isn't to cast judgment because they don't know a better way. They haven't been taught differently, so they go with what they know.

The religious spirit appears several times in the Bible, but we will examine a few verses from Mark 7. I recommend you go back and read the whole chapter. For now, we will focus on verses 9 through 13.

> *He was also telling them, "You set aside the commands of God, in order that you may validate your own tradition. For Moses said, 'Honor your father and your mother,' and, 'He who speaks evil of father or mother must be put to death.' But you say if anyone tells his father or mother, 'Whatever you might have gained from me is korban (that is, an offering to God),' then you no longer permit him to do anything for his father or mother, making void the word of God with your tradition that you've handed down. And you do many such things." Matthew 7:9-13 TLV*

It is stated here that they were adding to the law, making their own laws, and just putting God's name on it for creditability. That's what is going on in many, many churches today. You may ask what the harm is in adding to God's law if it isn't bad. I'll give you two reasons why:

1.) Scripture says not to add or take away from God's word.

> *"Now, O Israel, listen to the statutes and ordinances that I am teaching you to do, so that you may live and go in and possess the land that Adonai the God of your fathers is giving you. You must not add to the word that I am commanding you or take away from it—in order to keep the mitzvot of Adonai your God that I am commanding you." Deuteronomy 4:2 TLV*

2.) If you believe what man added to God's word, then you are getting a distorted view of God, and if you believe in a God that isn't the one true God of the Bible, then you aren't saved.

> *"For if you confess with your mouth that Yeshua is Lord and believe in your heart that God raised Him from the dead, you will be saved." Romans 10:9 TLV*

If you confess with your mouth that Jesus is Lord, but you have a distorted idea of who He is, then you don't truly know Him, and you aren't saved. You are believing a false gospel. That's the danger! It grieves me to know that many people are walking around feeling confident that they are going to Heaven when, in fact, they are going to Hell. This is one question you can't afford to get wrong!

"But understand this, that in the last days hard times will come— for people will be lovers of self, lovers of money, boastful, arrogant, blasphemers, disobedient to parents, ungrateful, unholy, hardhearted, unforgiving, backbiting, without self-control, brutal, hating what is good, treacherous, reckless, conceited, lovers of pleasure rather than lovers of God, holding to an outward form of godliness but denying its power. Avoid these people!" 2 Timothy 3:1-5 TLV

I really love how Jeremiah Johnson said that the religious spirit holds to an outward form of godliness but denies its power. They look and sound like God, following the "rules," but deny His power. If you deny His power, then you deny Him. He commands us to avoid these types of people!

"But woe to you, Torah scholars and Pharisees, hypocrites! For you shut people out of the kingdom of heaven. For you do not enter yourselves, nor do you let those enter who are trying to go in." Matthew 23:13 TLV

The devil has deceived so many people into receiving a gospel of being nice and kind instead of a gospel of righteousness. It is like the dream I mentioned. They thought just being "good people" was enough.

That's why reading the Bible for yourself is best and not taking anyone else's word as gospel. Not even mine. Go back and read your Bible alongside this book so you can compare and ensure that what I am stating lines up with the scripture.

The religious spirit was one of the main spirits that had Jesus crucified. Think about it. They killed Him because He wasn't following their laws and traditions, and He was going against the rules that they were trying to force on the people, laws that God never stated. If Jesus exposed them, they would lose power and credibility, so they had to get rid of Him. Little did they know it was all part of God's bigger plan for us.

According to Google, cessationism is a theological belief that certain spiritual gifts, like speaking in tongues, prophecy, and healing, ceased to be actively used by the Holy Spirit after the apostolic age, meaning they are no longer present in the church today; essentially, the miraculous gifts associated with the early church are not available to Christians today.

That has Religious Spirit written all over it. Of course, the devil doesn't want you to believe in those things because he gets his power from people believing that misplaced theology. The Bible never states that spiritual gifts ceased to exist.

I wanted to address what bondage means. According to Strong's Concordance, bondage is to subject, subdue, force, keep under, or bring into bondage. The enemy wants to subdue you, force you, and keep you under his rule by deceiving you into clinging to religion. He wants you to cling to your sin rather than Yeshua, to this world rather than His Kingdom.

"So lay aside lying and "each one of you speak truth with his neighbor," for we are members of one another. "Be angry, yet do not sin." Do not let the sun go down on your anger, nor give the devil a foothold." Ephesians 4:25-27 TLV

I want to share what the Lord showed me about giving the enemy a foothold in your life. A foothold is a secure, strategic position from which one can advance. I had to bind a book for my children one morning because they were starting a new homeschool novel study. I went to my closet because that's where the machine and supplies are. While there, I was sitting on the floor and verbally complaining about a situation I was dealing with. Talking out loud to myself sometimes helps me organize my thoughts. I didn't shut the door all the way, which I didn't notice at first. While complaining, the A/C turned on, and my door opened just a bit, but it caught my attention, interrupting my complaining. I immediately heard, "You are giving the enemy a foothold! What you see in the natural is exactly what is happening in the spiritual!"

I didn't even notice that the more I complained, the angrier I got. I stopped complaining, and I'm so thankful the Holy Spirit pointed that out for me. I do not want the enemy to have an advance over me because of the words that came out of my own mouth! There is power in the tongue!

"Death and life are in the control of the tongue. Those who indulge in it will eat its fruit." Proverbs 18:21 TLV

Do not give the enemy a foothold any longer to keep you in bondage to the spirit of religion. It is time to walk in the freedom your Heavenly Father freely offers you.

Because there is power in the tongue and what you say matters, if you feel led, pray this prayer over your life. Say it over and over if you must. Say it slowly. Whatever works for you. When you pray, do not doubt that the Lord won't move on your life. He loves you so much! When you are praying, all of Heaven is paying attention. Remember that!

Pray Out Loud:

Father, thank you for revealing this knowledge about the religious spirit. I can see where it has influenced me my entire life. It is time for me to wake up! I am ready to be set free and walk in the fullness You have for me. I want to experience Your freedom. I lay the lies, traditions, and beliefs that are not from You at Your feet. I believe You are who You say You are. You are the King of Kings and Lord of Lords, The Mighty Creator, God Most High, and I trust You and You alone.

Forgive every way I have sinned against you, others, or myself. I release it to you, Father. I receive Your forgiveness. In the name of Yeshua, I repent and renounce every opening, known or unknown, my ancestors or I have given to any spirit of religion in my family line. I repent and renounce every spirit of religion, and every work of darkness connected with it. In the name of Yeshua, I repent and renounce all legalism, traditions, and religious formulas.

I repent from mocking or gossiping about those I have seen in my life that I have thought were too radical in their faith. I want to be radically on fire for You, Lord. Thank you for forgiveness, mercy, and grace. Thank you for loving me, Father. In Yeshua's mighty name, Amen.

Chapter Four

What Fruit Are You Producing?

Suggested Reading: Galatians 5 & John 15

"But the fruit of the Ruach is love, joy, peace, patience, kindness, goodness, faithfulness, gentleness, and self-control—against such things there is no law."
Galatians 5:22-23 TLV

We will talk about fruit—not apples and bananas, but spiritual fruit. It comes from the Galatians passage if you have never heard of that term. Look at the end of that verse. It says that there is no law against such things. That's good news!

The fruits of the Spirit are character traits that come from the Holy Spirit because of our relationship with our Heavenly Father. Those fruits do not come from you. They can't be earned or worked for. They come from the Holy Spirit. The fruits are love, joy, peace, patience, kindness, goodness, faithfulness, gentleness, and self-control.

A Spirit-controlled person is always in full control of their own mind, body, and words. The fruit doesn't grow like regular fruit. You are not getting seeds that will grow into love, peace, patience, kindness, goodness, faithfulness, gentleness, and self-control in a year or two. It was downloaded into your Spirit as already mature fruit. You just need to learn to walk in it. The closer you get to your Heavenly Father, the easier it will become to show love to that driver in the car who cut you off, to be patient with a customer who is taking their time, and to have self-control when you just don't want to. It will come naturally to you.

How do we attain the Fruits of the Spirit? For that, we will head over to John.

"I am the true vine, and My Father is the gardener. Every branch in Me that does not bear fruit, He takes away; and every branch that bears fruit, He trims so that it may bear more fruit. You are already clean because of the word I have spoken to you. Abide in Me, and I will abide in you. The branch cannot itself produce fruit, unless it abides on the vine. Likewise, you cannot produce fruit unless you abide in Me. "I am the vine; you are the branches. The one who abides in Me, and I in him, bears much fruit; for apart from Me, you can do nothing. If anyone does not abide in Me, he is thrown away like a branch and is dried up. Such branches are picked up and thrown into the fire and burned. "If you abide in Me and My words abide in you, ask whatever you wish, and it shall be done for

you. In this My Father is glorified, that you bear much fruit and so prove to be My disciples." John 15:1-8 TLV

What does it mean to abide in Yeshua? In the Strong's Concordance, abide means to keep fast, together, abide, close, join, pursue, dwell, and remain in. Pick which one stands out to you the most. "Remain in" stands out to me. No matter what happens, I will remain in the Lord. No matter what the enemy tries to throw my way, I will remain in the Lord.

As you see in John 15, you cannot produce fruit unless you abide in Him. There will be many moments in your life when you will experience and live out the fruits, but these moments will always be temporary and conditional. I don't think you can fully understand what walking in the Fruits of the Spirit feels like. It is like a different level of freedom and living. It isn't out of your reach. It is attainable.

The opposite can be said for the fruit that comes from the religious spirit. The fruit of the religious spirit is quick to anger when people don't conform, and it is controlling, always looking for an argument, prideful, and judgmental. There is no evidence of love, peace, patience, kindness, goodness, faithfulness, gentleness, and self-control. The religious spirit will contaminate your fruit from the Holy Spirit. The religious spirit's purpose is to stand in the way of the Spirit of God's true work.

"The fruit of the spirit wasn't intended to be a list of goals for us to produce – it is the Holy Spirit through us that produces fruit." Dan Kimball

"Watch out for false prophets, who come to you in sheep's clothing but inwardly are ravenous wolves. You will recognize them by their fruit. Grapes aren't gathered from thorn bushes or figs from thistles, are they? Even so, every good tree produces good fruit, but the rotten tree produces bad fruit. A good tree cannot produce bad fruit, nor can a rotten tree produce good fruit. Every tree that does not produce good fruit is chopped down and thrown into the fire. So then, you will recognize them by their fruit." Matthew 7:15-20 TLV

In conclusion, by abiding in Yeshua and by keeping your eyes fixed on Him, you bear the Fruits of the Spirit. You can abide by scripture and not be abiding by Christ. You can read scripture and memorize it cover to cover, but if you aren't following Yeshua, they are just words on a page. The Words have to saturate your heart. We are talking about your relationship with Him here.

Start paying attention to the fruit you produce and the fruit from those around you.

I'm sure if you think about it right now, you can tell which fruit the people in your life produce. Seek your Heavenly Father to learn how to produce His fruit, not the world's. One is full and plump, while the other is rotten and covered in decay. It's your choice to make.

Pray Out Loud:

Father, help me produce good fruit. Give me the opportunity to love, have peace, be patient, and show kindness, goodness, faithfulness, gentleness, and self-control. Thank you, Holy Spirit, for these gifts with which there is no law against.

Holy Spirit, help me always remain in Yeshua. No matter what happens in my day, I choose to put Him first in all things. Keep my mind and heart focused on Him. In Yeshua's mighty name, Amen.

Chapter Five
Lukewarm Christianity

Suggested Reading: Romans 6 & Revelation 3

"As I see it, a lukewarm Christian is an oxymoron; there is no such thing. To put it plainly, churchgoers who are 'lukewarm' are not Christians. We will not see them in Heaven." Francis Chan

I was not going to add this chapter, but I feel it would be a disservice to you if I didn't. Please don't skip it because you may be walking on the lukewarm line and don't even realize it. I didn't know I was lukewarm because I didn't know better. Religion taught me I was doing enough, but sadly, I wasn't. There is no judgment here. The religious spirit wants you to believe you are saved, but what if you aren't? What if your church is teaching you a false gospel that makes you think you are saved, but you aren't? This isn't a question you should guess. You need to know where you will spend your eternity. I wish someone had taught me this when I was a kid. It would have saved me a lot of heartache and time.

"I know your deeds, that you are neither cold nor hot. Oh, that you were either cold or hot! So because you are lukewarm, and neither cold nor hot, I am about to spew you out of My mouth." Revelation 3:15-16 TLV

What does it mean to be lukewarm? According to the verse above, it is someone who isn't hot or cold for God. You are in between—one foot in the world and the other in God. You may ask what's wrong with that.

Jesus willingly left Heaven to come to Earth to die a horrible death and take your sin upon Himself.

"What shall we say then? Are we to continue in sin so that grace may abound? May it never be! How can we who died to sin still live in it? Or do you not know that all of us who were immersed into Messiah Yeshua were immersed into His death? Therefore we were buried together with Him through immersion into death—in order that just as Messiah was raised from the dead by the glory of the Father, so we too might walk in newness of life." Romans 6:1-4 TLV

One night, I was in my prayer room after reading Romans 6:3, which left me in tears. It shifted everything that I knew about Yeshua's death. Abba gave me a beautiful yet powerful vision of what that looked like, and I feel I need to share it with you.

He brought me to an empty tomb that was covered by a big stone. I was lying on the floor, wrapped in white bandages. I was covered in scars, blood, wounds, bruises, and dirt. I went through a rollercoaster of emotions. I was all alone in that tomb for what felt like forever, and then I looked over and saw Yeshua. He was lifeless, lying next to me. He was wrapped in white and was completely clean. Out of nowhere, I heard the verse, "Do you not know that all of us who were immersed into Messiah Yeshua were immersed into His death?" That's when the black spots, which represented my sin, started to move off of me, and I watched them one by one slide across the floor onto Yeshua's body. Then, the scars, blood, wounds, bruises, and dirt that were on me started to disappear. I looked at Yeshua excitedly to tell Him I was clean, and that's when I saw all of it on Him. He was covered in wounds, dirt, and blood. I could see a tear in His eye. The stone rolled away at that moment, and I heard a voice say, "You Are Free!" I sat up and looked at Yeshua and broke down crying because I didn't want to leave Him there alone and was asking Him why He took my punishment. The voice said again, "You Are Free! Go be with your Heavenly Father!" I could hear love in His voice. I'm crying just while reliving that moment to share it with you.

That's what He did for you and me! He willingly sacrificed His life. It is deeper than just a baby in a manger.

Lukewarm Christians can't sit through more than an hour of church, they can't serve or participate in outreach because they have errands to run or need to catch up on their favorite TV show. I'm being silly, of course, but I hope you get the point I'm trying to make. These are some of the excuses I have heard my whole life, and I have used the same excuses.

When you put other things, worldly things, above Yeshua, you are essentially telling Him what He did on the cross wasn't enough for you and that your desires are more important than His sacrifice.

"Then Yeshua said to His disciples, "If anyone wants to follow after Me, he must deny himself, take up his cross, and follow Me. For whoever wants to save his life will lose it, but whoever loses his life for My sake will find it." Matthew 16:24-25 TLV

Character Traits of Lukewarm Christians:

-lack of passion for prayer and worship

-lack of interest in reading scripture

-rarely sharing their faith

-justifying sin

-obedient when it works for them

-keeps faith separate from daily life

-No conviction

-prioritizing worldly desires

-inconsistency in church attendance

-prioritizing personal comfort over biblical truth

As discussed in the last chapter about the fruit of the religious spirit, it makes sense why so many Christians are lukewarm.

I saw this saying once that said God does not accept lukewarm Christianity. It repulses Him when we treat faith as nothing more than fire insurance.

If anyone wants to follow Yeshua, you MUST deny yourself, deny your worldly desires, and follow Him. I like how biblestudytools.com explains taking up your cross. Taking up our cross means sacrifice, laying everything on the altar. It's not a half-hearted commitment; it is a full surrender to God's terms of discipleship. It's a choice to live out the truth that we are "crucified with Christ," even if it means shame, rejection, or persecution.

> *"...and it is no longer I who live, but Messiah lives in me. And the life I now live in the body, I live by trusting in Ben-Elohim—who loved me and gave Himself up for me." Galatians 2:20 TLV*

I pray your eyes and ears are open to this truth. It is a hard pill to swallow, but God isn't too far away from you if you identify as lukewarm. He is right beside you, waiting for you to return to Him. He will never leave you.

> *"Chazak! Be courageous! Do not be afraid or tremble before them. For Adonai your God—He is the One who goes with you. He will not fail you or abandon you." Deuteronomy 31:6 TLV*

Pray Out Loud:

Father, thank You for never leaving or abandoning me when I have gone astray. I recognize my life has become lukewarm, and I am ready for change. Let the Holy Spirit take over. Thank you, Yeshua, for dying on the cross and washing me clean in Your blood so I can approach my Heavenly Father in such a way and hear from Him. I am not too far gone. You have not disowned me. I am made new because of You. I love You, Father. In Yeshua's mighty name, Amen.

Chapter Six
Final Thoughts

I PRAY THIS BOOK has helped you walk in freedom and that you learned something new about your Heavenly Father and yourself. I trust that the Lord exposed some root beliefs from which He plans to heal you. Let Him! I encourage you to get plugged into a Bible-based, Holy Spirit-led church and read your Bible daily. Spend time daily with the Lord in your secret place—your car, closet, living room, wherever you can be alone with Him. Just sit with Him and enjoy His presence. The secret place is within your heart.

"He who dwells in the shelter of Elyon, will abide in the shadow of Shaddai." Psalms 91:1 TLV

"But you, when you pray, go into your inner room; and when you have shut your door, pray to your Father who is in secret. And your Father, who sees in secret, shall reward you." Matthew 6:6 TLV

I want to close this book out by praying for you:

Abba Father, thank you for the person reading this book. Thank you for putting this book in their path. You see their heart, and You know the pain and trauma they have been through. You are Jehovah Rapha, the Lord Who Heals. I am asking You to heal their heart. Heal them from the pain that religion has caused. I know it breaks Your heart to see your children hurting and being deceived. They are taking back their life and giving it fully to You. Holy Spirit, lead them. Lead them away from fleshy desires and help them hear Your voice. Quiet all the other voices in their mind so they can hear You more clearly. I pray they long to spend time with you, Father. The secret place becomes the non-negotiable, and they can't live without it.

Sitting in your presence is what they can't live without. Help them to remain in You every day. This life isn't easy, and we were never meant to do it alone. You are our helper and comforter. Comfort and lead them today and every day. Help them to continue to walk in Your freedom. Thank You, Yeshua, for giving Your life for ours. I pray for a special blessing over their life. As they read these words, Your presence is coming upon them, and the Holy Spirit is touching their hearts. Cover them, Holy Spirit. In Yeshua's mighty name, Amen.

Quick Scripture Reference:

1 Timothy 1:18-19

Romans 14:11-12

James 1:6-8

Job 33:15-17

Acts 2:17

John 10:27

Matthew 7:21-23

Deuteronomy 4:29

Psalms 42:2

John 14:26

1 Corinthians 14:2

Mark 16:17

Matthew 10:7-8

2 Timothy 1:7

Matthew 7:9-13

Deuteronomy 4:2

Romans 10:9

2 Timothy 3:1-5

Matthew 23:13

Ephesians 4:25-27

Proverbs 18:21

Galatians 5:22-23

John 15:1-8

Matthew 7:15-20

Revelation 3:15-16

Romans 6:1-4

Matthew 16:24-25

Galatians 2:20

Deuteronomy 31:6

Psalms 91:1

Matthew 6:6

Invitation

IF YOU HAVE NEVER accepted Christ as your Lord and Savior, and you would like to, I want to give you the opportunity to do so now.

> **John 3:16: "That God so loved the world, that He gave His one and only Son that whoever believes in Him shall not perish but have everlasting life."**

> **Romans 3:23: "All have sinned and fall short of the glory of God."**

> **Romans 6:23: "For the wages of sin is death, but the gift of God is eternal life in Christ Jesus our Lord."**

Romans 10:9: If you confess with your mouth the Lord Jesus and believe in your heart that God has raised Him from the dead, you will be saved" (NKJV).

So, let's pray out loud!

Heavenly Father, I repent of my sins. I believe that Jesus died on the Cross for my sins and that You raised Your Jesus from the dead on the third day. Jesus, I ask You right now to come into my life, make me clean, make me whole, make me new in You. I am turning from my old life now so that You can use me as You will. Holy Spirit, fill me up. Come in and show me how to walk in Your ways. Guide me all of my days. Keep me on the narrow path. Lead me in the Way everlasting. May I walk worthy of the call You have placed on my life. Thank You, Jesus, for saving me. Amen.

Date I gave my life to Jesus _____

I want you to know how excited I am that you said **YES** to Jesus! This is **THE MOST IMPORTANT** decision you will ever make. Your name is now written in the Lamb's Book of Life! (Rev. 21:27, Luke 10:20). The Bible says in **Luke 15:10, "Likewise, I say to you, there is joy in the presence of the angels of God over one sinner who repents."** You are now a part of God's family, and I want to be the first to say, personally, welcome to the family!

About the Author

Heather Evans

Heather Evans is a Christian Life Coach and homeschooling mom of three. She was born and raised in Lake Charles, LA. Heather is passionate about helping Christian women heal from past trauma so they can experience inner healing, which often inspires her work. Heather holds a certification in Christian Life Coaching from the International Christian Coaching Institute. She enjoys reading, writing, singing, dancing, and spending time with friends and family. Heather is also actively involved in her church, Revival Culture. Currently, Heather resides in Orange, TX, where she lives with her husband, three children, two dogs, five cats, and several goats and chickens. You can follow Heather on Facebook and Instagram or visit her website at www.heatherevanscoaching.net.

www.ingramcontent.com/pod-product-compliance
Lightning Source LLC
Chambersburg PA
CBHW060956120626
46557CB00003B/1188